THE 10 BIGGEST BUSINESS MISTAKES

THE 10 BIGGEST BUSINESS MISTAKES

AND HOW TO AVOID THEM

PATRICK BURKE

WELLSPRING

North Palm Beach, Florida

wellspring

Copyright © 2020 Patrick J. Burke
Published by Wellspring

Cover by Snap Advertising
Interior by Madeline Harris
Typeset by Ashley Wirfel

ISBN: 978-1-63582-224-3(hardcover)
ISBN: 978-1-63582-233-5(e-Book)

10 9 8 7 6 5 4 3 2 1

Printed in the United States of America

To my late parents, Walter and Dorothy Burke,
whose moral guidance and impeccable example
helped me avoid the big life mistakes . . .
the ones that truly matter.

CONTENTS

FOREWORD

I love helping clients make more money running and selling their businesses. Fortunately, I have always had the facility to visualize transactions. This has helped me put together many deals for myself and my partners. More important, it has allowed me to help hundreds of clients start, buy, run, grow, and sell businesses of all sizes with tremendous success.

Two of the most successful of these are a diversified real estate services company with $500 million in sales and a medical consulting company with $60 million in sales. I helped both these businesses get started thirty years ago, each with less than $2 million in first-year sales. For the past twenty years, I have been lucky enough to serve on both companies' boards and have consequently been directly involved in multiple acquisitions and divestitures ranging in size from $2 million to more than $100 million.

In choosing the $8 million size of Tim's transaction I had two considerations. The number had to be reasonable in light of his original $2.45 million purchase price (see my book *Exit Velocity*). The amount also needed to represent a number that most business owners could relate to. Add or subtract a zero and I lose the owners of very small and very large businesses. Also, based upon my experience in wealth management, most investors believe $8 million will allow them, absent a profligate lifestyle, complete financial freedom.

So, whether your company is worth $800,000 or $80 million, the same ten mistakes must be avoided.

PROLOGUE

Tim woke up, looked lovingly at Laura, his wife of forty years, and assessed his feelings. *Fulfilled* was the first word to come to mind. Today was the day his business lifetime would profitably conclude. Looking back he thought of his successes and his failures. Fortunately the former not only outnumbered the latter but also far outweighed them financially.

Tim worked hard, envisioned the future, and made changes when needed. Nothing extraordinary, he thought, except he avoided the big mistakes. As he walked to the kitchen to start coffee for Laura (he preferred tea), he was counting the near-catastrophes he'd avoided during his long journey from disgruntled employee to successful business owner.

Drinking his tea as he admired the view of the Ohio River Valley from his back deck, he realized that number was ten. Ten times he had avoided a big mistake.

Years ago Tim's accountant told him business was like weekend golf: Winners avoided the big mistakes. Although Tim's 25 handicap would indicate he was never skilled enough to apply this concept to his golf game, the $8 million that he was to be wired today for his company, RCM, was proof he was skilled enough to apply it in spades to his business career.

Each chapter in this book will outline how Tim, a mostly fictional character, through good luck and experience avoided the ten big mistakes. My analysis follows.

1. MISTAKE ONE: Buy or Start the Wrong Business

I had just experienced the worst workweek ever as the CFO of Cincinnati General Hospital. Patient count and reimbursements were down. We'd also lost some key physicians to hospitals in Boston and San Francisco; it was a true Black Friday. On Saturday, I called my friend Jake, a well-known Cincinnati business broker, and told him it was time for me to hang up my eyeshade and buy my own business. Being a top-flight sales guy, he quickly sent me a link to two local businesses and one franchise opportunity he represented.

The two local businesses were small job shop manufacturers that appeared a bit down-at-the-heels. The franchise opportunity, the Trashinator, was really interesting to me. The franchise sells franchisees a truck with an articulating boom in the bed. At the end of the boom is a giant steel cylinder with spikes welded to it. The cylinder rolls over primarily construction dumpster trash, packing it down and resulting in fewer trash hauls. Brilliant in its simplicity, I thought. And, I had to admit, their mascot—a Terminator-like giant with spiked cylinders for hands—was very cool. I told Jake I was interested and to forward the franchise disclosure document. I was pushing forward. My attorney, Jim, had reviewed and okayed the documents and I had gotten approval from my bank for 80 percent of the $400,000 buy-in I needed to augment my $160,000 cash contribution. I couldn't wait to start smashing trash in the three-county territory my deal covered. I was proud of how far I'd taken this deal on my own and called my next-door neighbor Mike, who was also my one-man board of advisers, to report.

His first comment was, "Oh my gosh, Tim. I hope you haven't signed anything yet."

"No . . . other than the confidentiality agreement," I replied.

"*Whew!* That was close!"

"You sure sound less than enthused, Mike."

"On the contrary, I can with tremendous enthusiasm state . . . don't do it!"

"I got the money, the franchise is financially viable, and this is a good market . . . so what's wrong with the opportunity?"

"You're a smart guy," said Mike, "so I'm sure everything about the Trashinator checks out. But that's not the problem—you are."

At this point I had my Irish up and responded defensively,

"So you think I'm smart, just not smart enough to run my own business?"

"No, it's not that," he said. "It's just this is the wrong business for you."

I asked him why.

"Look," he replied. "You and I have had many discussions about finding just the right business to start or buy."

"I know. Those were great discussions and I recall you were pretty positive on franchises because—and I think this is a direct quote—their systems and processes create the holy grail . . . the sustainable advantage."

"Exactly," Mike said. "However, just because the business is sustainable doesn't mean you can maximize its value. You're a CPA by trade and for the last ten years you've been a hospital CFO. Nothing in your background indicates you have anything special to bring to construction trash."

"Okay, but why is that important?"

"Tim, think about it. If all you add is the ability to follow the franchise guidelines, your background in finance and health care is essentially wasted. You'd be better off finding a business where you're either the best player at the key position or second-best player at several positions. Most of the Trashinator's business would be construction related so, for you, it would be like starting over, practically from zero."

After calming myself with a few deep breaths I told him he was right. "I guess I wanted to move on so badly I was overlooking the obvious," I said. "This business, although a good one, doesn't really fit me at all."

"You got it," Mike replied. "Hang tight, we'll find the right one soon. Until then, keep your powder dry."

Of course, I did find it: RCM. And since I hadn't done this deal, I had the time and capital I needed to make RCM happen—thank God!

OVERVIEW

Throughout this book, we will discuss the sustainable advantage, which is the most critical element in a business's continued success. This sounds simple but it's not. Think about the local restaurateur; we'll call her Sue. She decides to expand from one to three locations and then shortly thereafter is back to one location, or maybe even none. Her first restaurant had an advantage; most likely it was her. Perhaps she was not only a great chef but also a great hostess and promoter. Her first restaurant thrived because it was the perfect stage for all her talents. Each successive restaurant got off to a great start because she was present . . . for a while. Over time the restaurant she abandoned in favor of the next one experienced a significant decline in guests. Within a couple of years she was back to her original location, poorer but smarter.

So what was the problem? She, like many entrepreneurs, was the advantage. Sue was the unique value proposition of her business, and as a result, her business was neither sustainable nor scalable because she was neither sustainable nor scalable. Many if not most small businesses are (or at least start out as) personality cults. There's nothing inherently wrong with that, but as with Sue, a cult is not sustainable. The moral: If you're buying a business, make sure the Sue problem has been solved. If you're starting your own business, create "Sue-like" processes that allow others to be "surrogate Sues," so you can successfully scale.

Look at the success of the big names in the quick service restaurant industry. McDonald's, Chick-fil-A, Wendy's, and Starbucks are businesses whose success is wholly dependent upon the consistency of the food, service, and customer experience. None of this is left to chance. All aspects of the business are completely spelled out in the policies, procedures, and resultant metrics the franchisor promotes, teaches, measures, and enforces. That's why the burger you buy and the service you receive at a Wendy's in San Diego is exactly the same as in Cincinnati. It's the opposite of a personality cult. It's an enforced sameness that is a result of proven procedures. Scalability and sustainability are not left to chance—they're ensured.

Everyone knows you shouldn't go grocery shopping when you're hungry; you'll end up with a basket full of Twinkies. Similarly, you shouldn't be searching for a new business when you're struggling with your job. You'll likely end up paying too much for the wrong business, which would likely be just the beginning of your troubles. Take time and assess your strengths and weaknesses to ensure you choose a business that fully utilizes your personal and business attributes.

DO YOU HAVE WHAT IT TAKES TO BE AN ENTREPRENEUR? TEN THRESHOLD QUESTIONS

I covered the question of whether or not you should own a business completely (and entertainingly, I might add) in my business parable, *Exit Velocity*. In the first chapter of that book, I outlined the ten questions that would-be business owners must answer before moving forward:

1. Can you live with the uncertainty associated with running your own business?
2. How would you rate your tolerance for risk?
3. What's your relationship with your money?
4. Can you lead people?
5. Are you competitive?
6. What's your work ethic?
7. Are you a good listener?
8. Can you sell?
9. Do you have a skill that adds real value to your new business?
10. Do you have a financial goal for your business?

I'll assume you passed that test, so we can move forward to finding you the correct business to start or buy.

DEFOG YOUR MIRROR

Tim's potential foray into the trash business indicates that he, like many people, failed to do a thorough self-analysis before buying or starting his own business. It seems pretty basic, but you should start with what you know. Although experience may not mean expertise, prior work experience in an industry means you have pertinent skills, industry knowledge, a network, and most important, a deep understanding of your customer base.

I don't generally support navel-gazing, but knowing and following your passion makes perfect sense. Owning and running a business is difficult and consumptive work, so having a passion for your product and customers will convert your work into your mission—which is what it needs to be. Further, truly believing in your product means that promoting it is not selling, it's giving customers the opportunity to buy what you know is a superior offering. Your passion for your solution will be palpable. The result should be a superior operation and higher profits.

Running your new business means living with a certain level of uncertainty. That doesn't mean you must eat risk for breakfast. However, understand where you fall on the riverboat gambler–actuary continuum and let that be your guide to the correct business. For example, service businesses require less capital and are easier to modify if the market changes than, say, manufacturing businesses. Existing competitors are a good indicator that a certain business makes sense and, perhaps counterintuitively, is therefore less risky. Blazing new trails is risky and costly. Only about 20 percent of businesses fail because they are outcompeted. Twice that number fail because there isn't enough demand for their product or service.

WHAT'S YOUR GOAL: JOB OR ASSET?

In chapter two we will contrast the difference between growth businesses which are run for value and lifestyle businesses which are run for income.

If you believe a lifestyle business, with its reduced risk and financial commitment, is the correct choice, you now must determine whether the demands of your chosen lifestyle business are a fit for you. For example, if the business will require significant travel or client entertainment and that's not your thing, then move on. Also, when you're the owner of a business, the buck always stops with you. So if handling a customer emergency at an inconvenient time is not a strength, don't opt for a hands-on, last-line-of-defense business. Believe me, if your business isn't a vocation and you're not absolutely driven to delight your customers, they'll find someone who is.

In order to determine the ideal business for you to own, the first and most important step is to discern your why. Your why could be as simple as creating a job to earn a living or as complicated as creating a wealth-building opportunity for both you and your children. Creating your job requires only a lifestyle business. A multigenerational business, on the other hand, requires the elusive sustainable advantage. Far different goals require a far different screening process.

WHOM DO YOU LIKE?

An important but often overlooked aspect of choosing a business is deciding whom you want to work with on a daily basis. This goes for coworkers as well as customers. I had a client, Larry, who was given a free minority interest in a business by a private investor. The business plan called for creating a chain of dry cleaners. Larry was great with customers because they were, in his parlance, his kind of people. However, his fellow workers, a mix of new immigrants and blue-collar tough guys, were decidedly not his kind of people. Two years in, with only three stores open, the investor decided Larry wasn't his kind of person and, as they say, they went their separate ways.

ROLLING THE BUSINESS DICE

Deciding between a start-up and an existing business depends on what sort of risk you tolerate best. If you're comfortable with financial risk, buying an existing business is likely the best route. Although this typically requires more up-front cost, it's less risky than starting from scratch. With an existing business you can analyze prior results and build an accurate forecast so you'll know exactly what you're getting into, even if you don't necessarily know the result. You may even be buying a product or process that, while established, hasn't been fully leveraged. This may offer the upside of a start-up without all the risk. Start-ups, by contrast, generally require less up-front investment, so financial risk is initially lower. However, they have far higher execution risk. Blazing new trails with a new product or service being offered to an unknown customer base is tough sledding. Your yield may be huge . . . or not. Either way, your investment of time and effort will definitely be huge.

BAGGING YOUR QUARRY

The idea that the right deal will find you if you make it known you're looking for a business is a fable. Finding a good business to buy or start is a full-time, multi-month undertaking. Patience will be rewarded. Mining your existing centers of influence is your first step. Lawyers, accountants, bankers, and insurance agents all know hundreds of business owners. Asking this group to introduce you to their colleagues will geometrically expand your search. As you'd imagine, the first question you'll be asked is what you're looking for. The second is how much you're willing to invest. Be prepared with definitive answers for both. These are busy folks, so don't assume your search will be renting a prime location in their brains. Keep in touch with periodic email updates and be sure to let them know when you do buy or start your enterprise.

Taking out a classified ad or adding a post to your Facebook page detailing your qualifications and what kind of business you're seeking may sound crazy, but I've seen it work. There are business owners who have not formally gone to market but may be spurred to action after seeing your ad or post. This could give you first crack at a great deal on a great company.

Business brokers and their bigger brothers, investment bankers, always have inventories of businesses for sale. Brokers generally represent smaller businesses (however, I have seen some fairly sizable deals come from business brokers). Investment bankers generally represent larger businesses. These larger enterprises are likely to be purchased by either strategic buyers in the seller's industry or private equity firms. These buyers are sophisticated and extremely well-funded; as a result, they're tough to outbid.

I suggest looking at a few represented businesses because the sellers are motivated and organized, and the process will give you a taste of the steps involved in an acquisition. Analyzing the businesses' information with your advisers, determining a price, and preparing a letter of intent will take your sophistication level up significantly. If it's the right opportunity, you'll move on to negotiating an asset purchase agreement, obtaining financing, and finally closing on your new enterprise.

2. MISTAKE TWO: Lifestyle

It was a Friday afternoon and we had just closed a huge deal with Stanford University Medical Center. I was on top of the world. Unfortunately, my drive home took me right past the Porsche dealership. And there it was, my dream car, sitting right out front, a Carrera 4S coupe, silver with red interior. I couldn't resist. I pulled in, got out of my aging Lexus sedan, and began walking around the Carrera. This of course resulted in a salesman materializing. "Beautiful," he said.

I responded, "Perfect; my dream car and dream color."

He said, "Want to take it for a spin?"

I replied, "Of course." And off we went.

It was even better than I'd dreamed. Fast, responsive, and turning heads everywhere we drove. Once we were back at the dealership, the hard sell started: "Great price, last of the 2020s, gone soon . . ."

I succumbed, even though $119,000 was at least twice what I'd ever paid for a car and exactly what I paid for my first house. I signed the papers and drove my Lexus, which now seemed jalopy-like, home. As I was pulling into the driveway I saw my neighbor Mike talking to his landscaper. He saw me, strolled over, and asked, "Why the Cheshire Cat grin Tim?"

Before I responded a pang of guilt came over me. "Just bought my dream car. So I guess the grin is appropriate." I told Mike about the big sale and the great deal on the car. Neither of which removed his scowl.

Finally he said, "Tim, you told me last week there was an acquisition you'd like to make. How do you square this car with that acquisition?"

"I can't, I guess. . . . It's just I have been working so hard. I wanted to reward myself."

Before I continued dissembling, Mike lectured me about the big mistake of treating a growth business as a lifestyle business. He convinced me, based on RCM's excellent track record, that the risk of not reinvesting was significant because it may cost us the next big growth opportunity.

I walked into my house, got on the phone, and canceled the contract on the car. We made the acquisition with very little bank debt. The result: We acquired an organization that's now our largest and most profitable business line. Clearly a better investment than a silver Porsche!

OVERVIEW

There is nothing inherently wrong with a lifestyle business. It makes perfect sense to start or buy a business that makes enough money for you to be comfortable and have a good work-life balance. Lifestyle businesses are also great if you want to take guilt-free time off for family or hobbies. The problem occurs when a business could be a growth business and *should* be a growth business but instead is starved for cash because the owner is treating it as an ATM. It is very difficult to have a steady-state business. If you're not growing you're likely shrinking, and there's a competitor who, sensing your weakness, is ready to eat your lunch. This is particularly true if the business you're treating as a lifestyle business is competing directly with other growth businesses. Think about the local pizza place trying to compete with a Domino's franchisee.

A good lifestyle business coupled with smart investing will result in financial security, but not real wealth. Real wealth results from building a growth business with a sustainable advantage that can someday be sold at a high multiple of earnings.

So, even though there is much more pressure in operating a growth business, the rewards can be far larger and can, post-sale, result in a truly lavish and leisurely lifestyle. You know, the power of deferred gratification and all that.

Your business is essentially a vehicle that is able to take you certain places, or in some instances, everyplace. If it's the lake for a weekend, a lifestyle SUV works fine. If it's Paris for the weekend, a growth-business Gulfstream III is required. Your business, your choice.

GAMBLER OR ACTUARY

There is an element of risk with all businesses. For example, if you own a shoeshine stand you will have low capital expenditures and no employees, but a rainy day means no sales. Although I would not equate business risk with going to the casino, there is one similarity: You must decide how much you're willing to bet. Some gamblers increase their bets only if they are winning and "playing with the house's money," while others are willing to dig deep into their pockets even when the cards aren't falling their way. Deciding where you fall on the risk continuum is one of the determinants of whether your enterprise should be a lifestyle or a growth business. Creating a sustainable and scalable business often takes more time, capital, and risk than many entrepreneurs can tolerate. And that's okay. Limiting the growth of a business to reduce risk is an appropriate value judgment. Clearly, not all business owners are riverboat gamblers, nor do they need to be. However, in my experience many entrepreneurs end up with lifestyle businesses not because of an aversion to risk but for an entirely different reason—namely, their own lifestyle.

SHOW OR DOUGH

Many business owners starve their businesses of necessary attention and capital because they've succumbed to the temptation to spend too much money on themselves and too little time on their businesses. This results in an enterprise that does not reach its full potential. Owners who become too enamored of exhibiting the trappings of the success of their businesses end up trapped in unsuccessful businesses. Often, when I talk to business owners who have fallen prey to this temptation, they respond with, "I need to reap the rewards of my hard work; I deserve it. I got into business to make money and I want to spend it." All that may be true. However, spendthrift owners must understand there is significant risk to starving their business of needed capital. This risk includes aggressive competitors who are properly treating their business as a growth business and will be impossible to compete with over time.

SELF-WORTH

If you are the owner of what you know is a growth business, you need to begin your cash planning by determining your paycheck. If you're the owner of a start-up, it's easy to figure out your pay; it's whatever is left in your checking account at the end of the month. This likely goes without saying, but as an owner you must pay yourself out of profits, not sales. As your business grows and becomes more profitable, it is important that you determine a fair compensation for yourself. If you take too much, you risk slowing growth; if you take too little, your self-inflicted poverty will itself become a distraction.

W-2 VS. ROI

The best policy is to pay yourself reasonable compensation. This figure is a function of your location, size, industry, profitability, access to bank financing, and ongoing need for capital expenditures. Of course, included in your compensation are your perks like car expenses, health insurance, and retirement plan contribution.

In addition to your time and effort, you must also be fairly compensated for your risk. Profits are your reward for the risks you've taken. This may seem obvious, but you're not really making money if you aren't taking profits out of the business. If you fail to pay yourself fairly for your risk, you may end up overpaying other employees out of your profits.

It's likely that your business will be structured as an LLC or an S corporation (these are known as flow-through entities). This means that profits are reported on your personal tax return. As a result, it's often hard for owners to distinguish compensation from profits. However, your CPA can help you determine when it's appropriate to distribute a portion of the business's profits in addition to your fair compensation. As with so many business questions, the answer is more art than science. It is important that you wear neither a hair shirt nor a cashmere jacket.

CASH IS KING

Although it may seem counterintuitive, you can retain too much cash in your business. A rapid accumulation of cash can not only indicate success, it can also indicate underinvesting for growth. If you've accumulated earnings to help fund growth, that's great. It will result in lower debt and may prevent a need for outside capital investors later.

One sure way to preserve cash is to properly utilize debt. A corollary to the "cash is king" maxim is using long-term debt to fund long-term assets (like machinery) and short-term debt to fund short-term assets (like inventory). Without the proper use of debt, it is impossible to know when or how much cash can be safely distributed.

Businesses may rely on sweat equity in the beginning, but sweat won't keep the lights on, much less shining brightly. The most sophisticated companies not only prepare an operating budget, they also prepare a detailed cash forecast. This includes forecasting the need for additional capital expenditures (including creating a hurdle rate for return on these investments) as well as working capital to fund any necessary increase in inventory or accounts receivable.

However, once the cash need is determined, it is appropriate to distribute the excess to yourself. Use this cash to build a diversified portfolio outside of your investment in your company. This is essential as a hedge against additional risk you may need to take on later.

3. MISTAKE THREE:
Professionals

I was waist-deep in my negotiations to buy RCM when my good friend and lawyer, Gene, made a surprise visit to my house early on a Wednesday night. After some brief pleasantries he said, "Tim, I can't in good conscience continue to represent you in your deal."

I replied, "Really, Gene? Is there some conflict of interest or what?"

"No, I'm just not qualified. You're not buying a simple business. Your financing will be complicated and health care information is subject to a bunch of regulations I know nothing about. Trust me, it is time to upgrade to a transaction lawyer at a bigger firm. You'll need expert representation to close and ongoing specialized advice I just can't provide."

"Wow," I said. "I really hadn't thought all that through. I guess I didn't know what I didn't know."

"I get it," he replied. "It's easier to stick with your current advisers, but you now need experience I don't have. It's not fair to you for me to learn on your nickel. And as much as it pains me to say this, Laura is equally unqualified. She is a great CPA, but her specialty is personal taxes and small business. I already discussed this with her and she agrees. It is time to align yourself with larger firms with more experience and expertise in transactions, particularly in health care."

As I was nodding my head I was also having a bit of an out-of-body experience. "So do you and Laura have anyone you could refer me to?"

"We thought you would ask that, and we both agreed on the duo that should be helping you through this," Gene said, handing me two cards. The lawyer was Jim Williams and the CPA was Paul Griffin. "We took the liberty of setting up a meeting with all of us on Friday morning at Jim's office."

On the wood-paneled elevator heading to the twenty-second floor of the Great American Tower, I was overcome with what I suppose was "pre-sticker shock." I didn't feel any better when the door opened directly into a reception area, meaning Jim's firm occupied an entire floor of this building. Gene and Laura were chatting with Paul, whom they introduced. As I was shaking hands with Paul, Jim entered the lobby, introduced himself, shook my hand, and led us to a conference room with a spectacular view of the Reds' stadium and the Ohio River; it was all quite intimidating. After Gene and Laura presented a synopsis of the work done to date, Paul began ticking off how his firm could handle the financial due diligence, as well as develop a request for a proposal to be submitted to both banks and mezzanine lenders.

Jim followed this up by explaining how he would approach the tax, business, and risk issues in the asset purchase agreement. He also explained his role in dealing with the lender.

Later as I rode the elevator to the lobby, I made the decision. I thought to myself, although Paul and Jim's presentation was great, it was all just too much. I would talk to Gene and Laura and convince them to stay in the deal with me. Then it hit me. Trying to convince them to stay on when they were advising me to change advisers was in essence giving them advice on something I knew little about, and it was contrary to their advice. I called Gene on his cell; he was still in Jim's office discussing some aspect of the deal. He took the call and I agreed to hire the new team.

OVERVIEW

The following message is being brought to you by a practicing CPA, and as such is totally biased. However, that doesn't mean it is not true. Having the best professional advisers will help you run a successful enterprise and make acquisitions properly with all documents properly drafted, risk issues covered, and tax consequences fully understood. The value of an experienced and sophisticated team of advisers grows geometrically with a business's size and complexity. As mentioned in the prologue, one of my common advisory themes is that the successful operation of a business is much like a weekend golf match in that the winner is the one who makes the fewest mistakes. Good advisers know what works, aren't afraid to tell you exactly what to do, and hold you accountable when you ignore their advice. There is no reason to continually learn from your own mistakes when you can draft off professionals who can prevent them. You should always be willing to pay for and follow great advice. Paying for advice is a capital investment in a valuable piece of mental machinery. The return on investment will be outstanding, and unlike an actual machine, it will become more productive and valuable over time.

Business is tough, complicated, competitive, and fun. The real fun comes from knowing you're fielding your best team against your competition. Your best team isn't just the folks you work with daily, it also includes your professional advisers. Too often companies are highly selective when it comes to recruiting employees, particularly the executive team. They pay up to attract and retain great people. However, when it comes to hiring professionals, price is often the number one consideration. In almost forty years as a professional adviser, I can count on maybe two hands and a foot how many times I have been asked my hourly billing rate. That's not to say I don't get asked what a client should budget for a certain service. That is a very common and proper question. As for the hourly rate, it's not really relevant if the value is there.

Choosing your professional team is every bit as important as choosing your business partners. I refer to professionals as spigot partners because you can turn them and their related costs on and off as needed. Great advice at the right time will always help you avoid the big expensive mistake. Just as a great business partner enhances your company's profitability, your professional team will save your company multiples of their fees.

A STITCH IN TIME

The very best time to develop a relationship with your professionals is well before you need them for a major transaction. This is particularly true of lawyers. Developing an ongoing relationship will result in better representation, lower fees, and more value because they need not be reeducated about your enterprise every time a legal matter arises.

The best way to find your team is through a personal referral. In addition to this "social proof," you should also find out exactly what the referred professional did for your contact and make sure it mirrors your needs.

THE BEAUTY CONTEST

Once you have gotten a few names, take time to interview the candidates. Just as with a business partner, your chemistry needs to work. You will be confiding in this person often, so the relationship should be friendly, not just cordial.

You also need to discern if your professional is highly

responsive and not merely reactionary. A good question here is: What was the last matter you handled in which you added unusually high value? If their response shows the adept handling of a small issue before it became a big mistake, you can move on to the next level of inquiry.

Experience with companies of similar size in your industry and market is mandatory. Having your professional team doing on-the-job training on your dime adds significant expense and leads to unnecessary mistakes.

At both CPA and law firms, you should meet all the members of your team. However, be sure that the adviser you choose will be your primary point of contact. As you analyze the firms, you will need to decide the pond question. Since your company will at least initially be a small fish, what size pond do you want it to swim in? This is especially true of law firms. Although large firms can handle any matter, you must weigh this against the fact that in a large law firm your company is unlikely to be an "A" client and as such may not be a priority. This is less of an issue with CPA firms since apart from the Big Four, they tend to be smaller but often have a high level of talent and expertise.

You don't want to run into Tim's problem and be required to upgrade as you begin to think big. Pick advisers who have dealt with companies that have grown significantly under their guidance. Ask for references from companies they have helped with typical growth issues. These would include capital raising, adding subsidiaries, acquisitions, and divestures. Your advisers should be experienced businesspeople who can help you create and implement a business growth plan. Having starters on your team who have been there, done that and have the T-shirt is critical to dodging mistakes and growing profitably.

You should also ask probing questions about your professional's personal characteristics. Beyond superior technical skills, you want a highly responsive professional with the highest moral character and an impeccable reputation.

YOU GET WHAT YOU PAY FOR

Of course fees are important. But as with all things, value is far more important than cost. In my experience fees are an issue only when there is a lack of understanding up front. If your professional is to bill you hourly, you should know in advance what a project will cost and be advised if there is going to be an overrun. If you and your professional agree to a flat fee, it needs to be fair to both of you. You don't want to be overcharged, nor do you want to receive less than the best service because a flat fee is too low. Also, make sure you agree on what the flat fee covers up front. It's impossible to predict every issue that your professional will need to handle on your behalf. As with hourly billing, if the matter is outside the flat fee, insist on a good estimate of cost before work commences.

4. MISTAKE FOUR:
Partnering

Note: Unnecessary and inappropriate partnering is costly and unfortunately pervasive—so much so, I have written about it twice before: in chapter five of Exit Velocity, *which is summarized here, and in the book* There Is No Us in Business.

Shortly after I purchased RCM, Linda, the CPA who had brought that deal to me, asked to join the company. We struck a deal and she came aboard. She did a fantastic job getting a new service line (clinical documentation improvement) off the ground and scaled profitably. This was no mean feat and was critical to the growth we needed to fund our acquisition debt. Linda had agreed to a bargain salary but had negotiated incentives that quickly got her to market rate compensation. She was a critical member of our team, a model employee, and an effective leader.

At the time I hired Linda she had asked if she would have a chance to buy in once she had proven herself. My response, being caught somewhat flat-footed, was between positive and noncommittal. Eight months into my first year of business, after Linda had signed a few large hospitals to sizable deals, she asked to buy into my company. Although she was a great employee and had added extraordinary value to our business, I neither needed the capital nor believed it was the right time to add a partner.

I took the question to Mike. I told him I felt somewhat trapped. Although I hadn't given Linda the right to buy in as part of her employment contract, I didn't want to disappoint her, reduce her effort, or completely foreclose the idea. Certainly there was a possibility that I would need capital later for acquisitions. Mike explained to me the gold standard for taking on a partner: A business owner should bring someone in as a partner only if that person possesses a skill that is absolutely critical to the success of the business and that skill cannot be acquired for money alone.

Clearly, Linda's skills, although very valuable, didn't meet Mike's ultrahigh standard. So I felt good about not accepting her offer. Mike also suggested I take the conversation down a different path and find out why Linda was so keen on the idea of buying in. As I had predicted, turning her down proved to be a tough discussion. However, I learned that her primary reason for wanting to buy in was to have a wealth-building opportunity beyond her own investments and our company 401(k) plan. Instead of selling her equity, I instituted a stock appreciation plan, which allowed her to share in the growth in value of the company at no cost to her. And as an added bonus, it didn't dilute my ownership.

OVERVIEW

Entrepreneurs are by nature an independent and confident lot. They're confident in their skills, ideas, and ability to execute. However, for some reason these lone wolves often convert to pack animals when they start a new enterprise or buy a business. The cool, analytical entrepreneur who has thought through all aspects of her business often starts tossing equity around with little or no regard for its value.

Business isn't doubles tennis—you don't immediately begin looking for a playing partner. It's more of a triathlon, in which you perform all aspects of the business as you compete with your opponents. You may need a bike mechanic or a swim coach, but ultimately it's your performance that determines success. From the outset, you should treat the equity in your enterprise as your most valuable asset. If you don't believe it will be, you shouldn't be starting or buying a business. With that in mind, and applying cool logic rather than emotion to the partnering decision, most entrepreneurs decide to go it alone. The result: higher return on their time and capital, and most important, a happier owner.

As mentioned, taking on unnecessary partners is such a common and costly mistake, I devoted an entire book to it. Reactions to the book have ranged from "Oh come on, partners can't be that bad" (from the uninitiated) to "Why didn't you write this ten years ago?" (from the experienced entrepreneurs). I'll let you guess who has it right.

THE GOLD STANDARD

As an adviser to business owners for four decades, I can say with great authority that improper partnering is far more common than proper partnering. The likelihood of fulfilling the precise needs of a business at a certain time with someone you already know is very low. Most often the person you bring in as a partner will fail to add value commensurate with his ownership. Conflict generally ensues. A costly buyout and even more costly dissolution are common outcomes.

Many if not most entrepreneurs start businesses because they are confident in their ideas (many), work ethic (strong), and risk tolerance (high). Add to this self-confidence and an overall high opinion of themselves, and it's no wonder entrepreneurs fail to appropriately match when they engage in "business bumble." As explained by Mike, the gold standard for choosing a partner is finding someone who has a non-buyable and essential skill. Swapping equity for a skill you could pay for with cash is almost always a poor trade.

For most entrepreneurs who are buying or starting a business, there's likely a sizable skills gap. Unless you're going to be operating a really simple business, like a shoeshine stand, it's likely there are plenty of essential tasks you can't or don't want to do. However, you should exchange equity for a skill only when it's absolutely, positively necessary. Say you're a really talented and successful real estate investor who is approached by a national retailer to build, own, and lease back stores in locations throughout the country. You're probably very comfortable with assigning value to the property and putting together the lease terms. However, site location, design, construction, management, and finance are likely outside your wheelhouse. Landing someone with that sophisticated skill set plus experience with a national retailer may require offering equity.

UNDERSTAND THE WHY

Even if a person meets the high standard, it's important to understand her why. Often the equity in your company, as with Linda, is important only as a wealth-building opportunity. If that's so, the need can be met with some sort of nonqualified deferred compensation plan. Stock appreciation plans like Linda's are a great example. These plans allow participants to share in the appreciation in the value of a company over a period of time. For example, a company valued at $5 million could adopt a plan that allows certain employees to receive 10 percent of the company's appreciation above this amount over the next 10 years. If the company's value, based on an agreed-upon metric, increases to $10 million during this time period, then participants would share $500,000. This amount is generally paid out over 5 years. Problem solved and you still own 100 percent of your enterprise.

LAST RESORT

As you'd guess, a business's need for money has put together more odd couples than a mail order bride service. This often occurs with a new business. However, it also may occur when an operating business either hits a sizable bump or lands an outsize opportunity that requires significant new capital. In any instance, partnering for capital should be your very last option.

The best-case scenario is to fully understand your cash needs in advance. A well-executed monthly pro forma presented cogently and professionally to your banker will yield your need for nonbank financing. Armed with this information, you can tailor your search to the most likely prospects.

The cheapest money is, of course, your own. If you decide to search for outside capital, you should be acutely aware that the size of your own investment in your business is the best evidence of your commitment and confidence in the enterprise to banks, suppliers, and other capital sources. I'll cover the many alternatives to selling equity to raise capital in chapter seven. In my experience partnering is rarely needed to finance a business unless it is a capital-intensive start-up.

FIND A "10"

If you've run all the traps and determined you absolutely must partner, then please choose wisely. The threshold question is compatibility. This doesn't mean you can't wait to swap philosophies over a bowl of fudge. Rather, your partner needs to match your passion for the business and, like you, be committed to continually upgrading his skills. I suggest all partners take a personality test like the DISC. This test will give partners great insight into exactly what makes each other tick. Perceiving business issues through your partner's eyes is an important step toward minimizing disputes, especially the existential ones.

Now is clearly the time to draft off of your lawyer's superior knowledge and experience. Make sure your employment and operating agreements thoroughly cover the waterfront. This will include tight noncompete covenants and thorough buy-sell terms. These two items, if fully covered, reduce the misunderstandings that cause most disputes. As you'd expect, the best time to deal with these potential problems is before they arise—and they will arise. Let your lawyer help you visualize the future of your business and the potential issues that may arise, and gain consensus now on how you will handle them, while everyone is still happy.

Last, and most important, your partner must be of the highest moral character. No matter how valuable or talented he is, if you can't trust him you're adding a level of uncertainty and stress to a situation that will already have plenty of both. If you wouldn't be proud to have your potential partner's name next to yours on a sign swinging in front of your business, you've made a poor choice. Never compromise; it's just too important.

5. MISTAKE FIVE:
The Wrong Team

My banker, Nick, had just left my office after reviewing my first year's financials. To say I was flying high would be an extreme understatement. I had exceeded my sales budget by almost 50 percent and had been able to prepay a portion of the high-interest seller note while keeping the bank and my payables current. Nick was exuberant in his praise and even asked me if I was interested in increasing the limit on my line of credit to make acquisitions.

My assistant, Meggie, interrupted my daydream of unbridled success to announce a call from a former coworker, Ben.

"Hi, Ben," I answered. "Good to hear from you. What's up?"

"Well, Tim, I just left my boss's office and, based on a recent downturn in business, he is laying off several members of the management team, including me."

"Tough break, Ben. You've been at Durmed for, what, ten years?"

"Yeah, came here right after my career in public accounting. It's been a great run. But the government cut reimbursement for home medical equipment, which has been devastating. I guess it's time for a new challenge. I know you're now successfully part of the for-profit medical community after your long stint in the nonprofit hospital world."

"Yes, made the leap about a year ago," I said. "Best decision ever. It's great being my own boss—and being justly rewarded, I might add."

"That's great, Tim. I guess by now you've guessed that I'm interested in whether you might have a spot for me at RCM?"

"Great timing. My banker Nick just left and he is thrilled with our first year's results. He is encouraging me to add to my management team. I don't know what your responsibilities included at Durmed outside of finance but I am looking for a CFO with some operating responsibilities. I guess sort of a CFO/COO hybrid. Do you think that's in your wheelhouse?"

"Absolutely," Ben replied. "Bit by bit I've added operational responsibilities to my CFO role. In fact, before the downsizing I was about to suggest we bring on a strong controller we could eventually promote to CFO so I'd have more time to focus on operations."

"Very interesting. I'd love to get together."

So we met up and I was just about to offer Ben a job when I decided to make two calls: one to his boss, Randy, the CEO of Durmed, who I had known from my hospital days, and one to Mike, my one-member board of advisers.

The call to Randy was interesting. Without him explicitly saying it, I got the strong impression Ben's dismissal was not 100 percent related to a business downturn. According to Randy, Ben's interest in operations was more a product of his dissatisfaction with his role and authority as CFO rather than any particular talent or skill managing operations. It seems Ben, although a good CFO, wore out his welcome with Randy by not staying in his lane. Still, Randy was more positive than negative.

Conflicted, I called Mike. After I described my predicament, he responded with his usual bluntness. "Tim, although I am not wholly against opportunistic hiring, it's a rare candidate that forecloses the need to undertake a search. Frankly, it'd be close to miraculous if Ben was a perfect fit for your CFO/COO hybrid. You've got a great little company that could attract top-level talent, particularly if you are willing to hire a promotable young gun and train her up. If I were you I'd take a pass. If you're serious about the position, create a detailed job description and hire a top-flight recruiter."

"You're right," I said. "I was putting too much reliance on my past relationship with Ben. I just figured he was someone I could trust. I'll follow your advice and get to work on the job description. Another mistake averted, thanks to you."

"No sweat," he replied. "The vast majority of business

owners are guilty of hiring too fast and firing too slow. They just don't have the sixth sense necessary to pick great team members. Infallibility complex is a common affliction among the newly successful. Don't believe the headlines— slow down and make all decisions as carefully as if you were still a pre-revenue start-up."

"Great advice. Once again, thanks."

OVERVIEW

Choosing the right team for your business is obviously critical. However, despite the importance of putting the right players in the right positions, most entrepreneurs get it wrong most of the time. Just as Mike said, the most common problems are hiring too fast and firing too slow. Why is this problem so common?

The problem of hiring too fast stems from what I, as a lifelong Cincinnati Reds fan, call the Pete Rose effect. Most entrepreneurs, like Pete Rose, are imbued with a super strong work ethic and boundless optimism. They truly believe they can transform employees, even those with below-average skills and drive, into valuable players through their excellent example and the sheer force of their iron will. This is patently not true. A good friend of mine, who had spent a lifetime in the human resource field, once told me that a person's basic nature can be categorized as true north, and the greatest amount of change that can be achieved is northeast or northwest. Entrepreneurs, however, believe they can take the employee all the way down south—which is pure folly.

Firing too slowly is partly due to the disbelief that the north-to-south conversion did not happen. However, this occurs mostly because entrepreneurs lack attention to detail, which is compounded by the general failure of entrepreneurs to see value in middle managers such as human resource professionals, who revel in the details. Whatever the cause, it's real, and entrepreneurs generally will not pull themselves out of this process until they understand their own limitations. See yourself yet?

PUNCH LIST OR PUNCH OUT

It took many years for me to realize I wasn't effective at interviewing and choosing good employees. Instead of getting good and pertinent information from the candidates, I did what I do best: sell. If I thought the candidate had even a 50 percent chance of being successful with us, I put on the full-court sales press. Having an oversensitive awkward meter, I also expended an enormous amount of effort making the candidate comfortable. Between selling and comforting, I rarely made an accurate assessment of the candidate's suitability for the position. I later corrected this by using a standard questionnaire, but I still fight my sales and comfort bias.

Before we cover what you should be doing, let's go over what you shouldn't be doing. First and foremost, hire what you need, not who you know. My first receptionist was my seventy-four-year-old mother. Unfortunately, she hadn't worked in an office in forty-five years. The result: dropped calls, angry clients, and a flummoxed mom. I moved on to my wife. After two days Mary Jo walked into my office and declared, "Either I'll be your secretary [which she was really good at] or your wife [even better than as a secretary], but not both." Easy call. So I poached the receptionist from my former firm, paid her top dollar, saved my marriage, and immediately professionalized my business. Disaster averted.

You may believe *disaster* is too strong a word, but it's not. The cost of the wrong hire is that person's salary. If you add lost productivity of the empty slot to the recruiting cost, that number is likely on the low side. The last thing any business needs is to incur an almost totally avoidable expense.

Instead of hiring be a stealth cost center, make hiring the *right people* one of your business's sustainable advantages. As with every other function a business performs, failure to develop a process results in relying on luck. And as with all processes, it is critical to first determine the purpose. That's simple: hiring the very best person available for your opening.

Step one in the process is to develop a thorough job description. This forces you to think carefully about the true needs of the business. This description needs to be fully disclosed to each candidate. I recently hired a tax manager who quit after four days. She said the work was beyond her skill level and that we didn't fully explain her client responsibilities. Since she had only ever worked for herself, we had no references to check and relied on her description of her abilities (which were overblown, as it turns out). Our fault, really.

Involving key employees in the hiring process is also critical. They will be great judges of fit and function. However, doing so highlights the need for standardized questions and scoring, so each person's impressions can be fairly compared. The answers should determine whether the candidate can handle the key aspects of her job. As in my own case, without a carefully crafted questionnaire, all you may glean from an interview is whether the candidate is particularly introverted or extroverted, but you'll learn little about suitability. Determine the skill level the position requires, develop a skills test, and review a writing sample. Don't rely on anecdotal evidence for a decision that is so important.

ACTIVE BEATS PASSIVE—EVERY TIME

Your processes should also include active recruiting. As a partner at an executive and legal recruiting company, I can attest to the fact that at least 80 percent of professionals would classify themselves as passive candidates. So although they are not actively looking, they are also not *not* looking. For some high-demand positions, your candidate needs to be literally pulled from a competitor's seat. Hire a recruiter rather than limit yourself to only 20 percent of the qualified pool.

In order to successfully recruit internally, you must understand this process is rarely as simple as calling candidates who qualify. The best candidates are almost always very difficult to find. The first step is going to someone you know who in turn may know someone who is either your candidate or knows your candidate. You'd like that first call by you or your recruiter to be warm. Obviously this is not only more art than science, it is also extremely time-consuming, hence the reason many businesses hire professional recruiters.

DON'T TRUST, VERIFY

As part of our recruiting firm's services, we perform exhaustive reference checks. These checks include forms that ask former managers to score the applicant's performance. These are valuable, but it's been our experience that the scores reflect at least a 25 percent grade inflation. It's also important to go beyond the candidate's named references to other employees within their former employer, perhaps at a lower level, who worked directly with the applicant. The truth is out there. You just have to work hard to find it.

We also perform background checks. We always ask applicants if such a check will reveal anything untoward. However, it's amazing how often certain things are "forgotten." Be careful. Although not everyone who had an issue in the past will continue to have issues in the future, you owe yourself every relevant data point before adding a member to your valuable team.

CULTURE

Since every company is also a team, your process must address more than just functional fit and performance and include inquiries that will determine cultural fit. The vast majority of new hires fail due to attitude rather than lack of skills. Clearly it's very common to be addicted to experience and hire mostly on "résumé skills." However, such skills should be weeding tools only. Attitude must be thoroughly assessed during the interview process. You need recruits to be excited about the company, the team, and their role. Motivation should be instilled before the first day of work.

Motivation will come naturally if a recruit connects strongly with the company's mission and culture. Because you'll be trying to set the highest possible tone during the recruiting process, you can expect some candidates to self-select out, and that's okay. What they've learned about your business may someday make them a customer or even an advocate.

Even if someone does not look great on paper, he may kill it in the interview. Generally this occurs because you've looked beyond his existing skills to see true potential. Get good at developing your own talent and divining hidden talent. This will help you field a better team and do it more cheaply. The need to continually recruit people with upgraded skills when you need them is expensive and time-consuming and should be mostly unnecessary if you can successfully "grow your own."

WELL BEGUN

The ability to properly recruit, train, and retain will result in your company becoming the employer of choice in your market. Adding a continual recruiting process will make it easier to attract the very best candidates and top-grade your team. Just like in pro sports, the best teams must continually change personnel to stay competitive.

You've recruited and hired the perfect candidate. You now need to work to retain them and optimize their value to your company. The first step is a fully developed onboarding process. This ensures employees know exactly what they'll be doing, whom they will be reporting to, and how they will be evaluated. It's also a great way to introduce the new hire to your company's culture. As with other company functions, failure to create an appropriate onboarding process complete with checklists and handouts will result in employees creating their own system—one you'd likely disapprove of.

GET THIS RIGHT

Although compensation may not be the most critical factor in an employee's decision to stay, it is clearly important. As a result, it is also important your compensation philosophy match your business's brand. If your brand is the premium service provider, your employees should be paid at the premium end of your industry's pay band. Otherwise, the people you have servicing your customers will not consistently hit the premium mark. On the other hand, if you're a "value provider," you'll need to compensate in the bottom half of the applicable pay band or your margins will suffer greatly. Information about your industry in your region is readily available from either your trade group or a local employer's research organization. Get the information and benchmark your company's compensation against the proper standard.

Great people need to see and believe that your company offers them a great future. Their future development should include opportunities for more responsibility, autonomy, and compensation. An obvious corollary is that your company must make a commitment to growth. If not, employees will see their career path blocked by more-senior people. The best and brightest won't wait for openings; they expect the company to continually provide challenging new positions to grow into. Developing effective strategies for profitable growth will help you challenge and retain your key players.

MADE TO MEASURE

Lastly, create a tight process for ongoing evaluation of each team member's performance. NFL teams grade every player's performance on every play. This is likely overkill for your business, but the more frequent, the better. Ideally, managers should provide some sort of evaluation at the conclusion of every significant project an employee handles. The need for at least yearly evaluations is obvious. This evaluation should focus not only on areas of improvement but also on instances when the employee shone. However, if you do this only once per year you are relying on memory, which generally emphasizes the negative and results in diminished opportunities for the employee's improvement. It's my experience that the evaluation session should be separate from the annual raise discussion. If they're combined the instructive aspect will likely be overshadowed by the financial aspect. The employee essentially forgets everything said except "the number."

6. MISTAKE SIX: Think Big

Our medical audit business was cruising along. Early issues with key clients, including the Cleveland Clinic and the Mayo Clinic, had been resolved. However, the writing was on the wall. The audit business would start shrinking as the commercial base, those patients covered by regular insurance versus capitated plans, shrank. We had started a fledgling business line providing medical coding assistance to mostly urban hospitals that had issues hiring and retaining medical coders because of their inner city locations. Our coder teams would fly in for a long weekend or two and catch a hospital up on its coded records. Although this was a profitable business line, because of the travel cost and the reluctance of many coders to travel, it was going to be impossible to scale.

Around this time I met Ed, a hospital linen salesman who wanted to work for us. Because Ed was a good friend of a board member, his interview process was really a series of conversations about the challenges of our business. As you would guess, our inability to scale our coding business was a prime topic. In our final meeting, just before I hired

Ed, he brought me a business plan to establish a remote-coding business. Since this was before the time of electronic medical records, the plan would entail hiring a software developer to write a program utilizing optical character recognition and the means to securely transfer a patient's record from the hospital to the coder (HIPPA regulations are extremely tight). The coder would then ascribe the appropriate payment codes based on the record and send the file back to the hospital to be submitted to the ultimate payer. Ed predicted the cost of the software would be $1 million and said he would be happy to head up this new undertaking.

This was a gut-check moment. After a thorough scrubbing by the board, we went forward. Ed was spot-on; the software development did cost $1 million. As it turned out, the 9/11 attacks caused a significant disruption in the travel-coder marketplace. This hastened the adoption of the remote-coding option by hospitals despite early misgivings about HIPPA security.

This "think big" move was responsible for 40 percent of my current revenue and has tripled the number of hospitals we serve—probably my best decision ever!

OVERVIEW

Even the biggest risk taker likely believes she knows when to "fold them." According to the late Kenny Rogers, that, along with knowing when to "hold them," is a viable life philosophy. Despite Kenny's sage advice, it's likely that most business owners would admit to folding early and losing a sizable pot. And maybe that's okay. We all have different levels of risk tolerance, and business needn't be a series of trials by fire. But some opportunities that can be very quickly scaled must be pursued. Few fall into the "must do" category, but there are opportunities that you know you can execute because they leverage existing skills. Add to this the possibility an opportunity will result in rapid growth and may even introduce your business to new and bigger customers and you realize you must move forward, particularly if these new customers would likely perceive your company as a valuable ongoing resource. If the new opportunity also results in your company providing a unique product or service, you'll have more pricing power and resulting margins. Moreover, executing on big opportunities will allow you to attract and retain higher-level people like Ed, who will continue to apply their ample gray matter to helping you grow your business.

Several years ago in my role as a volunteer fundraiser for a local charity I called on Bill, one of Cincinnati's largest and most successful real estate developers. His office had the standard ego wall with pictures of Bill with various famous people. However, the largest single item (larger even than the obligatory carved wooden eagle), hung prominently just behind his desk, was a quote from Johann Wolfgang von Goethe: "Dream no small dreams for they have no power to move the hearts of men." I had just finished a book about Frederick Law Olmsted, who designed Central Park and the layout of the Chicago World's Fair. I mentioned to Bill that this had also been Olmsted's favorite quote. He admitted that he had first seen it in connection with Olmstead. Bill, a religious man, said, "Although that quote didn't inform my whole life, it did inspire my largest and boldest developments." I'll admit that hearing that from Bill had a significant impact on me, and it should help inform your business decisions. Once your heart has been moved, you'll move the hearts of others.

DREAM BIG

A dream is by nature evanescent. Making it real requires persistence, optimism, hard work, and the ability to lead and inspire. Despite all the talk of income disparity, the American dream is not a zero-sum proposition. If you reflect, you will realize no billionaire ever took anything from you. In fact, one may have given you a job or a lifesaving technology. Stop worrying about others and work hard on your own big dream.

An excellent prompt for a big new idea is to determine the most important problem in your industry and figure out how to solve it. If you can do this you will have developed a unifying vision for the future of your business.

The founders of ConstructConnect, a Cincinnati-based company, learned that construction blueprints were one of the most shipped items by FedEx. The company developed a way to transfer blueprints online, thus solving a significant information-transfer issue. This in turn led to the company accessing and selling customers' industry-leading construction data, as well as offering best-in-class visibility of bidding opportunities for construction projects. Big problems are opportunities for big solutions, big pricing power, and big profits.

THINK BIG

If what you're doing is not leading you to your desired destination, you may be thinking too small. Delaying gratification is a hallmark of successful entrepreneurs. And studies have shown the ability to delay gratification is the number one indicator of success. If you're already a successful entrepreneur, you have the patience and persistence to execute on a big idea. Stop listening to the wrong people. Low-level thinkers concentrate on survival and security. You're capable of escaping this trap. Think bigger, get bigger, and achieve more. You'll be happier.

Even thinking big may be thinking too small. Transformational leaders think moon shots, like President John F. Kennedy's vision of sending a man to the moon. Apple's moon shot was built around two transformational ideas: reinventing the customer experience with their devices and building retail space that would actually enrich people's lives. There are now 758 million iPhones in use worldwide and 506 Apple stores in twenty-five countries. As with Kennedy's moon shot, mission accomplished. Upon returning from Italy, Howard Schultz told his partners at Starbucks they should start selling brewed coffee in their Seattle shops, which until then had specialized only in beans and coffee equipment. He rightly believed the big idea of selling coffee would lead to the moon shot goal of creating a place between work and home for their customers. Starbucks now has twenty-four thousand stores worldwide. Guess Schultz was right.

ACT BIG

Remember, every big business was once a small business. You need to expand your thinking. Thinking bigger, acting bigger, and actually getting bigger are three wholly different things. However, they must occur in that order. If you don't develop a bigger vision and establish and track concrete goals for sales, profits, or new outlets, bigness will not happen. The goals themselves must meet the BHAG standard (big, hairy, audacious goals). Once again, no small dream . . .

7. MISTAKE SEVEN: Close Too Soon

It was a Monday night. I was watching the Bears get walloped by the Packers at Lambeau Field. Sue, my wife, walked in and said, "Could you mute that for a minute? We need to talk." I did her one better and turned off the game (not mentioning, of course, it was a blowout).

"What's up?" I asked.

"Well, Kim wants to quit her job and move to West Palm Beach to help an acquaintance open three Pure Barre exercise studios. . . . That just can't happen."

I said, "It might be a good experience. Doesn't she have a friend she can stay with there?"

"Yes," Sue responded. "But that's not the point. If she moves down there she may never move back."

Although I was thinking our daughter moving to Florida wouldn't be so bad—we'd have a great place to visit during Cincinnati's dreary winters—I said, "You're right, we can't let that happen. You two are peas and carrots. You need to be close. What do you suggest?"

"Find her a business to buy or start. You're good at that, right?"

Accepting the challenge, I responded, "Okay. I'll talk to her and we will figure out something to do together."

And so it began. Kim and I opened Zephyr, a blowout bar, the second one in Cincinnati. Kim had seen Drybar and similar businesses thrive in New York and Los Angeles and reasoned Cincinnati could support at least two blowout salons. Well, there is a reason Mark Twain said, "When the end of the world comes, I want to be in Cincinnati because it's always 20 years behind the times." Between the "necessary" fancy build-out and funding losses, this endeavor was having negative consequences beyond taxing my patience. In addition, the combination of troubleshooting Zephyr and draining my personal savings was putting my business and personal solvency at risk. So, I sat Kim down and we had a tough conversation about Zephyr's viability. Her only competitor had closed, which she thought was great. I, however, wondered if that was a harbinger of doom. She said, "Dad, that salon was paying three times what I'm paying per square foot and it's in the wrong area of town. Please fund a few more months . . . and I'll add cuts to our service offerings." She had been balking at that because the blowout salons in other cities did blowouts only and not cuts. After a slight pause she added, "Dad, I know we'll make it."

She was right. Although the financial metrics were improving only slightly, the number of new clients was on a significant upswing. Within a few months the salon was turning a profit and repaying my investment. More and more Zephyr was establishing itself as a brand. Looking back, the shutter option would have meant 100 percent loss of my investment. Moreover, the chain reaction for RCM due to my need to replace this capital would have significantly reduced my risk tolerance. Clearly this would have led to a pullback, resulting in fewer business lines and a significant loss in RCM's value.

OVERVIEW

Much has been written about the quixotic entrepreneur who just won't give up, no matter the odds. Even when it's obvious the business just isn't clicking, many owners continue fighting an unwinnable battle (more on this later). Less is written about the owner who slogs through a protracted start-up phase because she rightly believes she has a great new idea—probably because great ideas that are slow to catch on are extremely rare. Trying to be first or even early to an idea is far riskier than adopting an existing business model. Here you should think of the home-exercise businesses SoulCycle, Peloton, and Echelon all of which have successfully followed the existing at-home exercise model. Still, it is possible, and the rewards are far greater if you're first and successful. As they say, if you can't be first in the category, set up a new category. This advice, however, should be ignored by most first-timers.

BUILD A BRAND

We all know the best companies, such as Coke and Rolex, are built around great brands. A successful brand is born when a company's products always meet or exceed customers' expectations. Essentially a brand is a company's promise that no matter the product, if it's part of our brand, customers' expectations will be met or exceeded. Brands are extremely tough to build because consistency is difficult to achieve. It requires dedicated people, systems for repeatable performance, and metrics to ensure the systems works. Most new businesses, particularly in a new category, fail to perform anywhere close to this level. However, when a business does manage to successfully create a brand, even though the business is not yet profitable, it should continue. A brand is the ultimate sustainable advantage and should be fully exploited. Building a brand is highly intentional. Brands are the opposite of a wish or a hope. They are instead the result of strict adherence to standards that ensure repeatable and superior products and services. So if you rightly believe you've built a brand, stick with the business. It will succeed.

LENGTHEN YOUR RUNWAY

As you'd expect, the most common cause of a business's early exit is lack of capital. Prior to opening a business, the owner should ensure he has the capital runway to not only gain momentum but also turn the tide in the event of an early slowdown. As painful as it may be, you need to work closely with your CPA to develop a cash forecast. There's no reason to start a business only to run out of funding before it has a chance of surviving on its own. But this happens all the time. Most entrepreneurs will predict and have funding for the first year's losses, but few entrepreneurs plan to lose money next year. In my experience businesses that run out of cash and lose early momentum rarely survive. Get it right the first time.

Once you've completed your forecast and solved for negative cash, you'll have quantified your need . . . maybe. Go back through your assumptions and make sure there is zero unnecessary spending. The usual culprits include too much space, too many employees, and too much and too expensive furniture and equipment. Once you've skinnied that up, the next step is bootstrapping. Pull out all the stops; leverage your suppliers and service providers by asking for liberal payment terms. Once all this is done, you will know how much cash you really need.

But will you really? A very common mistake among first-time business owners is the failure to understand pricing, which results in setting prices too low. If your marketing and sales plans work, there should be appropriate demand for your product or services, which in turn produces some pricing power. Remember, it's the marketer, not the market, that sets price.

PLEASE DON'T DILUTE

Now that all sources of cash flow have been wrung out of your model, your real cash needs are apparent. As discussed in chapter four, your first source should be another call to your bank. It could be that your cash needs coincide with a buildup in accounts receivable or inventory, which banks are happy to finance if your business is profitable. If that's not the case, it's time to look to your own finances. Stay within your own financial risk tolerance but figure out what you are willing to invest. If you and the bank are exhausted and you still need capital, then you'll need outside investors. The first group of investors are usually classified as the three F's: family, friends, and fools. These are nonprofessional investors you should insist lend money to your enterprise rather than buy into it. Repayment should be based on your business hitting certain performance bogeys. This ensures complete transparency and should prevent undue and unwanted meddling in your business.

Once you've tapped out the three F's, you've exhausted the sources of nonprofessional investors. The next group are those folks who, in exchange for their cash, expect to own a piece of your enterprise and have the right to later sell it, either back to you or to a third party, at a tidy profit. This may seem to be a lose-lose proposition because you're not only giving up ownership but also subjecting yourself to the scrutiny of a partner who you know is not in it for the long haul. Not so fast. It may just be that your idea is so big there is no way to properly and fully exploit it without outside capital. Remember, you may earn a much higher return owning 50 percent of a thriving business than 100 percent of a subpar operation.

Now that the cash piece has been solved, there are key operational steps to staying open and growing profitably.

FIND THE BULL'S-EYE

Once you've been through a few business cycles you will fully understand your market and your customers. It's now critical for you to cater to who you perceive as your ideal client. This gives you the correct standard for products and services, how your business should look, and even the feel of your advertising. Trying to sell to everybody will result in a significant waste of resources and an ineffective marketing and sales effort.

Having identified your ideal client, you now must ensure she knows who you are and how to find you. This is critical to building a durable brand. Lululemon pays to be on the correct corner in posh neighborhoods because that's where its clientele shops. Create a vibrant client community. Stay in touch with your clients. Send thank-you emails after their visits. Send surveys and use the information to improve service. Become the business of choice for your product or service. Make all this happen and the elusive power of premium-brand pricing is yours.

POLISH YOUR CRYSTAL BALL

You should also be prepared for the sophomore slump. There's often a sales plateau not long after the initial launch of a business. Through innovation, your business will have a window to offer a new product before the customer is lost. It's a good idea to have this phase two in your hip pocket before you start. Alternatively, the innovation may be a natural uncovering of a need based on your early experience with your customers. In either event make sure the capital and enthusiasm are available to successfully execute your next phase. If you're capable of doing this multiple times and can become a constant innovator, you have created a scalable and sustainable business—the holy grail.

If none of this works and you must close your doors, it's okay. Everyone who tries makes mistakes. Winners bounce back. And remember, it's just a business; it's not you.

8. MISTAKE EIGHT: Close Too Late

It was a good idea; I was sure of it. We had a great reputation with our hospital clients and had seen firsthand the often calamitous aftereffects of Epic and Cerner, the software giants of electronic medical record installations. These included confused staff, underutilization of the product, and general administrative dysfunction. The path forward was clear: We needed to find some talented IT consultants who were experienced with these software products, send them to our client hospitals, clean up the mess, get paid, and move on. We had always been able to successfully enhance our brand by broadening our service offerings with our customer base while maintaining quality. I saw no reason why we couldn't do it again.

We immediately set out to recruit the appropriate medical IT consultants. Even though we had never recruited for this skill set before and didn't have anyone internally to benchmark against, we confidently began hiring. Admittedly, the candidate pool and our resultant new hires were far different from our current team. First off, they were IT people who had developed medical expertise. Our folks, on the other hand, had all started in the medical field and later added to their skill sets. This fact should have alerted us to the likelihood of future issues but no, we moved forward blithely. The new IT people were a little more independent but not exactly renegades. We believed that with some effort they could be transformed. So we attempted to indoctrinate them into the "RCM way" while simultaneously dispatching them to our client hospitals who were begging for assistance in this area.

Quickly, several issues emerged. Because our managers had not worked with such an unruly bunch, they couldn't solve some basic but critical issues. Productivity varied wildly among the consultants, as did profit margins. Deliverables likewise varied based upon which consultant was providing the service, and not surprisingly, client satisfaction was all over the lot.

As with all past service delivery issues, we decided to throw big money at it. We established metrics, initiated standardized deliverables, and provided intensive training programs for the consultants. To properly market and sell this new offering, we completely revamped our website and hired two new salespeople. After two quarters we had invested $500,000 and there was no end in sight. Stan, my CFO, begged me to stop the bleeding. As bad as the return on investment was, the feedback from the hospitals was worse.

The service level and inconsistent results were clearly jeopardizing our relationship with our clients. Instead of listening to Stan, I doubled down. By December our investment had swelled to $1 million against revenue of only $300,000. Our impending year-end board meeting forced me to face facts. I realized I was protecting the IT product mostly because I couldn't believe that the combination of my business acumen and $1 million wasn't able to solve *any* problem, much less provide IT services to our loyal hospital clients. Although I had to wince when the board voted to cease operations, it wasn't because I harbored any belief that more time and money would make it successful; it was because I knew it wouldn't. I'd been wrong, but at least I shut it down before it jeopardized our other business lines.

OVERVIEW

We've all had the thought. "I can't give up now—I've put too much time, effort, and money into this." This is true whether it's a home project, a relationship, or a business venture. Of course, as they say in the law, past consideration is no consideration. The size of your investment is relevant only at the time it's made and later to determine the ultimate return on investment. It has zero bearing on success. The impulse to throw good money after bad to prop up a failing business is extremely common. In my opinion, this impulse has resulted in more business losses than any other factor.

We can all be intellectually stubborn, particularly as

it relates to our homegrown ideas. This is intensified dramatically when the idea has been translated into a business decision. It is turbocharged when this decision has resulted in a significant cash investment.

YOU CAN'T UNBURN A STEAK

We have all heard the disclaimer in advertisements for financial products stating that past performance is not indicative of future results. However, we also know this isn't true. Past performance is by far the best predictor of future results. Investors put great weight on a stock's price–earnings ratio, which is 100 percent backward-looking. Unfortunately, when it comes to business ventures, prior results and other obvious indicators of problems are too often weighed far less heavily than the amount invested. Totally illogical, but understandable. No one enjoys being wrong, especially when it involves losing money. As painful as shutting down a struggling business is today, it is far less painful than betting more money tomorrow on an obvious loser.

Entrepreneurs, although extremely passionate, are generally also extremely logical. As described in Edward de Bono's book *Six Thinking Hats* and borne out by my experience, entrepreneurs generally wear the yellow optimist's hat, concentrating on the benefits of a decision, and the white hat, seeking pertinent facts. This should result in decisions that are based on the sound evaluation of future gains, but it does not always happen. Although it is a well-known maxim that if you find yourself in a hole, you should stop digging, many entrepreneurs refuse to drop the shovel.

Everyone fears failure, and newly successful entrepreneurs who are just beginning their careers often believe in their own infallibility. As a result, they have a strong desire to stay consistent with their decisions. Admitting a venture, product, or service line is not worth more time and money is inimical to their overblown business self-image. It takes time to learn that no single individual is an endless source of great ideas. To believe otherwise is pure hubris.

The money already invested in a venture results in the ever dangerous sunk-cost bias and thus the tendency to continue investing in a losing proposition because of what has already been spent on it. Succumbing to this phenomenon results in not only throwing good money after bad but also not spending time and money on other, likely better opportunities.

ACCEPT FAILURE AND LEARN

Since sunk costs are irretrievable, it's best to act like you have only the present and the future—because you do. With that in mind, it's easier to detach yourself emotionally from your past decisions. The goal of all business decisions is to help create sustained profitability. However, this end often gets confused with the specific means to attain it because we become attached to the costs we've incurred on the means. Even though it's far easier to forget the details surrounding the decision to continue spending, we seem to always remember the cost. When it comes to sunk-cost bias the key is to simply be aware of it and the practically gravitational pull it possesses. Instead of dwelling on sunk cost, make a habit of accepting your mistakes and moving on. To continue to be a successful entrepreneur, you need to be fanatical about telling yourself the truth even when it's painful, and maybe even when it's harmful to your own financial reputation.

9. MISTAKE NINE: Sell Too Soon

Talk about validation—we'd been open for less than two years and already I'd received an offer to buy my business. Out of the blue a buy-side investment banker representing a local private equity firm, Hi Mark, called. The banker, after downloading what he knew about RCM, which was a lot, dropped the other shoe: His buyer was willing to pay a five multiple on trailing twelve months' EBITDA for businesses like mine. I did the math: $5 million; I was dumbfounded. I told him I'd get back to him soon. He said he'd be sending a nonbinding letter of intent the next day.

Still stunned, I called my mentor, Mike, and explained the situation, concluding with, "This is life-changing; I think I have to take it. Although five million doesn't provide my family a lifetime of financial freedom, it's darn close."

Mike paused for an uncomfortably long moment and finally said, "That's really interesting and also flattering." He left it there and ended our call.

After hanging up I had time to reflect on the call. It

was, I guess, unsettling. Mike obviously did not share my excitement.

The next day the letter of intent arrived and as promised, the offer was $5 million and included a provision about a guarantee of working capital. I emailed it to Mike and asked if he could call me that evening. He responded that he'd drop by around seven if that was okay.

When Mike arrived that evening, with almost no preamble he started in on me. "Look, I'm not denying five million is a lot of money—it is. However, there are a number of things you need to consider before you move forward."

I responded, "Let me get a soapbox. I've got a feeling I'm about to get schooled."

"Don't look at it that way, Tim. Here's the thing. A nonbinding LOI is just that. It's kind of a teaser to get you hooked on the idea of selling."

"Okay. So what's wrong with that?"

"Well, once you're leaning you're a little easier to topple."

"Not sure I follow," I said.

"Let me explain exactly how these things play out. First you get hooked on the number. Next you envision the number wired to your savings account. You sign the LOI and due diligence commences. Just like when you bought RCM."

"Due diligence was kind of pro forma for RCM, if I recall."

"You're right," he said. "It was. However, RCM was a

well-run mature-stage company then. Now with your new team and new products, it's more of an early-stage growth company. And you still have acquisition debt to pay off. Then there's the matter of the working capital requirement."

"Okay, give it to me straight. What exactly is going to happen if we move forward?"

"Hi Mark will send in their due diligence team, who will determine that because your people, processes, and metrics are not all in place for your new business lines, they are reducing the five million to four million. They'll justify this by claiming the need to restate your pro forma EBITDA by subtracting the cost of the additional infrastructure for your new product lines. This will likely reduce it from one million to, say, eight hundred thousand. That's just the subjective stuff. Their offer contemplates a cash-free, debt-free deal. So, although you can keep your cash, all of your long-term debt needs to be paid off, including the acquisition debt. Next, they'll insist you deliver working capital at its current level. As a result they'll be keeping all of your accounts receivable even though I know they far exceed your payables and accruals. I can tell by your face that you've done the math in your head, so what's the new number?"

I replied dejectedly, "Three point six million."

"It's just too soon, Tim. You're not close to what I believe will be the company's peak performing years. You have a lot of work to catch up your team and your processes on your new lines to the standards of your acquired business lines. As you know, only repeatable performance can scale. I've seen your numbers and you're not there yet. Hate to burst your bubble but you've got a great company, and if you continue to run it well you will have a great exit someday . . . just not today."

"So it's back to work, I guess?"

"Yep. The good news is, you're on someone's radar. The bad news is your blip is just not yet big enough."

OVERVIEW

I have a chair in my office I have written about before. I call it the BOB chair. This stands for Burned Out Business owner. The typical scenario: I get a call from a business owner I would describe as fairly successful. Most likely it's a business he started and grew, and although he has numerous employees, he manages mostly by himself. To make it simple, let's call him Bob. Bob comes in to see me, sits in "his" chair, and says, "I've had enough. I need you to help me sell my business. It's not fun. Sales and profits have flattened. My employees are driving me crazy and my personal life is in shambles."

If I were being glib I'd respond with "What kind of sadist would force that situation on someone else? And what kind of masochist would pay money to be put into that situation?"

My non-glib response is to tell Bob to think about his business as though it were a highly collectible vintage car.

Like vintage cars, great businesses are scarce, are in high demand, bring premium prices, and, properly cared for, will continue to appreciate in value indefinitely.

So although Bob may have once been driving an exquisite vehicle, he's now contemplating selling what might just be a heap. Clearly he's violating the old maxim of buy low and sell high.

SELL HIGH

It's certainly true that distressed businesses are sold every day. However, this is mostly to turnaround specialists who have a certain set of highly refined skills. Moreover, distressed companies are priced at a steep discount. Thriving businesses, on the other hand, always sell at a premium (if properly marketed). I tell Bob to run his business as if he'll need to sell it tomorrow, even if that is highly unlikely. To sell at a top price someday, he needs his business to consistently hit peak performance metrics. The idea that the price paid for companies is based on past performance is only partly true. However, the idea buyers will actually pay for tomorrow's potential is mostly wrong. By far, the most important data to a buyer is current performance and, based on the company's processes and metrics, how predictive that is of future performance.

Unfortunately, the correct time to sell a business is not necessarily related to when the business's value reaches the owner's "exit velocity" number. And although the "selling too late" phenomenon covered in the next chapter is more prevalent, the "selling too soon" syndrome is definitely real. A paradox, perhaps, but the best time to sell is when you absolutely don't have to. It's pretty hard to get the best price when your back is against the wall. Your company will hit its highest value when it's cruising along, making plenty of money and growing nicely with a strong team in place. Most sellers, as previously discussed, tire out before hitting this stride. Instead they go to market too early and fail to maximize value.

EXIT VELOCITY

Some of my most successful clients got into business with their exit velocity number mentally posted on their dream wall. They consistently made decisions they believed ensured long-term success and resultant durable value. Making a series of these "durable value" decisions for an extended period is necessary to achieve maximum value. For your company to hit this maximum value any time before year ten is unusual.

The persistence, patience, and perspective to correctly time your exit is fairly rare but still a worthy and attainable goal. If you believe your company is at maximum value, it's important you are extremely well prepared to defend your number. If you've asked your CPA to value your company (good move already), understand what the value drivers are and make sure you have them well defined and running smoothly. Even if the valuation is at or close to your number and you don't believe your systems will withstand the scrutiny of due diligence, it's too soon to sell.

AUCTIONS WORK!

The old saying "one buyer is no buyer" is absolutely true. If your company is too early in its life cycle to attract more than one potential buyer, negotiating will be impossible because the only alternative is no deal. I've seen clients waste months haggling with one buyer and in the end accepting either a number nowhere close to theirs or willingly walking away after draining themselves and the members of their staff. As you'd expect, performance suffered for months thereafter.

A little commercial here for business brokers and investment bankers: Although you should never lose sight of the fact that for brokers and bankers the real client is the deal and not you, in my experience they rarely take from your plate. The auction process ensured by their involvement consistently brings prices that more than pay their success fees. They know how to price and where to find the correct buyers.

KNOW THE MARKET

Next commercial: This is also a great time to rely heavily on your CPA and lawyer. Their involvement will minimize post-closing risk and taxes and maximize net proceeds. You just can't beat that combination.

To maximize value, you should understand the universe of possible buyers. Your buyer will likely be your direct or indirect competitor. You should understand your potential buyers long-term growth strategy so you know what will intrigue them. Past acquisitions are a great source of this intelligence. Armed with this knowledge, you can and should put your company in the bullseye of their acquisition target. An example is being a leader in a market that a competitor is about to enter. If you don't yet have this information or you do have it but know your company hasn't achieved this stature, keep at it.

GET BIG

Buyers like size. All else being equal, larger companies are more valuable not only because their earnings are larger but also because size commands higher multiples. If you believe you have the people and systems in place but haven't utilized them to achieve significant growth, it's too early to go to market. Deploy your internal assets, achieve scale, and then go to market. If you haven't yet put your systems in place and instead decide to try to convince a larger company that your ideas executed by their team will result in outstanding growth, you may sell but it will be at the buyer's price.

Entrepreneurs are a competitive group, so it's rare to see one sell out of fear. But it happens. Competition should have you tightening your chinstrap, not running off the field. There is always going to be competition. You should be worried only if competitors are truly decelerating your growth and you know you can't compete without linking up with a bigger, stronger company. Absent that, beating the competition should up your game and help you create additional long-term value.

BE AN ENVIRONMENTALIST

In addition to the variables you can more or less control, there are external variables that you can't control, that tell you it's too early to sell. For example, you would think an economic peak would be a perfect time to sell. Your business is hitting record sales and profits and value is high. However, the specific terms of your deal could spell problems. Although every seller wants an all-cash deal for top dollar, they rarely get both. Top-dollar deals contemplate long-term success, thus the buyers usually insist on a long-term payout. As a result, generally 30 percent or more of your sales price will be paid out over, say, five years. Moreover, the amount of these out-year payments are generally contingent on performance. If the economic forecast over the so-called earn-out period is negative, expect a haircut on your sales price. If the economy has been in a trough and starts to bounce back, you may still want to wait. Buyers believe, as mentioned before, your most current year's results are most predictive of long-term results. Thus your price will be depressed. Putting a couple of good years on the books before going to market is critical to receiving your best price. A good economic forecast post-sale makes receiving your full earn-out payments much more likely. Forecasting economic conditions is tough, but it's much easier than the folly of trying to call the top of the stock market. Keep your crystal ball highly polished!

READ THE TEA LEAVES

It's hard for owners to walk away at the correct time no matter what, but particularly if they don't have a plan for what's next. So if all the other stars are aligned and you don't have a concrete plan for your next thing, it is probably best to hold on to your company until you do. I had a client get his exit velocity number for his business and retire to Florida only to call me six months later to tell me that he had purchased a lawn service business. He just wasn't ready. In fact, a year later he moved back to Cincinnati, bought back his old company, and began running it again.

10. MISTAKE TEN: Sell Too Late

It was an opportunistic acquisition. One of RCM's friendly regional competitors in Chicago had clued us in to a small software company for sale. The company, Uptima, had developed certain algorithms that performed excellent quality control on hospital bills. The QC function resulted not only in correct coding but also in the hospital receiving the proper reimbursement based on its case mix. The price was right at five hundred thousand. The founder and her son, both of whom were critical to the enterprise, agreed to come aboard. The software was a boon. It enhanced the work of our remote coders, allowing us to charge a premium over competitors. Hospitals also purchased it as a stand-alone product to enhance their own coding. Installations were quick, mostly trouble-free, and very profitable. We had forecasted a low volume of hospital sales and were blown away by the quick adoption and explosive growth. Our CFO was ecstatic—quick sales, high margins, and best of all, because the software was subscription based, recurring revenue. Two years in we were approached by a buy-side broker representing a private-equity-backed health care SaaS (software as a service) company looking for an add-on acquisition. They really liked Uptima, but of course we did too. The buyer offered $3 million, which was seven times that division's earnings. Even though this would have been accretive to our value because the market would have valued us at a five multiple, we declined. Stan, our CFO, said to me, "We can't give up this cash cow. It produces our best margins and has the shortest sale cycle."

I responded, "You're right, and since it has an SaaS component I believe the halo effect increases our overall valuation."

Before dismissing the offer outright I ran the whole scenario by Dan, our chief information officer. With zero hesitation he said, "Take the offer."

"Why?" I asked.

"SaaS is not our core competency; it's a one-off. And rumor has it 3M is about to introduce a category killer in this space."

So we accepted the offer of $3 million, and 3M did introduce a great new product that, although not exactly a category killer, was a superstrong competitor of Uptima. Once again, big mistake had been avoided.

OVERVIEW

When Bernard Baruch, the early-twentieth-century financier, was asked how he had become so rich, he responded, "I made my money by selling too soon."

We've all heard the saying that you can stay too long at the fair. This is certainly true when it comes to your business. Often an owner, in an attempt to squeeze out a few more years of wages and profits, allows his business to lose its edge because, frankly, he has lost his edge. Those last couple of years of lax ownership may result in a loss in value many times what the owner was able to extract from the business during this period.

Although private companies don't trade on an exchange, their value, like that of traded companies, is determined mostly by their most recent performance. Owners who wait too long to sell often see the value of their company eroded not only because recent profits are down but also because buyers believe recent performance is most predictive of future performance. As a result they apply a lower multiple to the earnings in determining the company's value. Coupling this with the fact that the sales proceeds are taxed at the lower capital gain rate while the "extra" earnings eked out of the company are taxed at ordinary income rates results in a net cash double whammy. Great name for a band but a terrible result.

TIMING IS EVERYTHING

I have been advising clients for years not to pay for potential when acquiring a small business. I suggest that a seller's puffing about new opportunities, products, and services be countered with pointed questions about why these ideas haven't already been implemented. Notwithstanding this advice, it is tomorrow's results that are being purchased and sold. If diminished sales and profits are projected, the price will decline. Unlike publicly traded stocks, in which it's all but impossible to call the top, small business owners should be able to get close. As with everything else in business, having a detailed plan to "institutionalize" your company's value by creating sustainable profitability is critical.

Failing to sell a business at the appropriate time is not always and maybe not even mostly due to greed. As discussed, squeezing out a few more years of cash certainly ranks high when it comes to the cause for bad sale timing. However, a more common cause is the owner's identity being caught up in his business. I once had an owner, George, age seventy-five, accept an offer for 98 percent of his asking price and then call off the sale the day before closing. When I asked him why he said, "Where will I go and what will I do without my company?" Obviously not selling was an illogical and emotional decision, but it happens all the time. Unlike a professional investor or a private equity firm, who buy or start businesses with the intent to sell, most owners don't see the business in terms of a potential transaction. It's really more like a family member.

Another common cause of ill-timed sales is failing to understand business valuation science. A business's value, unlike a building's, will vary widely based on many factors, but mostly recent performance. I have worked with business owners who thought a ten-year-old business valuation done by a business broker (who generally has a vested interest in selling the business someday and therefore often overvalues the business anyway) was a sort of baseline. Unfortunately when the owner was finally ready to sell, near the end of her business career, she learned the value had seriously eroded. Just like stock market prices, private business prices are extremely dynamic. A fair but unexpectedly low offer often results in owners further delaying a sale, hoping for a much-desired business or economic turnaround—neither of which may be likely.

SUSTAINABILITY EQUALS SALABILITY

Most business owners and certainly all my clients have heard the advice to run their business every day as if they'd be selling it tomorrow. Unfortunately this advice is rarely followed. Most businesses fail to set up the proper processes, hire the correct people, or establish the proper metrics to ensure consistent performance. Such consistency is the sine qua non of sustainability and scalability, which is what smart buyers pay top dollar for. As you'd expect, creating this kind of highly disciplined business environment is a process and not an event. Business owners often believe they can fix problems right before the sale, but by then it's too late.

You can't own your business indefinitely. It will someday

be owned by someone or no one. Most owners fail to keep this fact front of mind. Instead they wait until their energy and passion are waning and then take their business to market. At that point the business is generally in decline if not fully distressed. Most buyers don't have the confidence, vision, or capital to buy a distressed business. As previously discussed, this results in a smaller pool of buyers (turnaround experts) and a lower price.

HIT THE PEAK

So when is the correct time to sell? That's easy: when the business value is at its peak. This generally occurs when the business has a strong track record of above-market sales growth coupled with an increasing percentage of that growth hitting the bottom line. It's also extremely helpful if the seller has enough gas in the tank to get the buyer off to a flying start by staying on for, say, two years. As a bonus, if you sell while you're relatively young, you have more time to reduce your overall financial risk by diversifying your investments, making it that much easier to take on the risk of starting or buying yet another enterprise.

If your business is a lifestyle business such that it is completely dependent on you for sales and services, it is essentially your "incorporated job." As such it's really not salable unless you find an apprentice. Failing that, you should run it for as long as possible and then shut the doors. And that's okay if it's what you set out to do.

EPILOGUE

There you have it, the ten biggest business mistakes and how to avoid them. There are clearly hundreds of others, but avoiding these ten will practically ensure your business goals will be achieved—goals I hope meet the BHAG standard. In my experience, setting and achieving bigger, hairier, and more audacious goals is no harder than achieving smaller ones. It just takes a little more planning, patience, and a willingness to redirect some of your raw entrepreneurial energy toward developing processes. Fighting the strong impulse to build the business bicycle while you ride it will be difficult, but if you're successful you'll have a far better ride to a much better location. I also hope I've been able to convince you that turning your business into a valuable and transferable asset is a matter of ensuring your business advantage is both sustainable and scalable—a tall but clearly achievable order that will have outsize consequences . . . like complete financial freedom.

POST-EPILOGUE

Dear Reader,

I know what you're thinking: "Okay, so that's the ten biggest mistakes—what about the other five hundred smaller ones?"

At Burke & Schindler, we not only know all about how to avoid mistakes, we also know proactive approaches to help you grow your business. Here are just a few of the ways that we have helped our clients build durable value:

- Establishing compensation plans that promote excellence
- Creating, tracking, and enforcing effective business metrics
- Building sales systems that promote profitable and sustained growth
- Executing strategies that ensure pricing power
- Constructing balance sheets that support a robust growth plan

By now I am sure you're interested. Call me and let's talk about having your company execute at the highest possible level.

Patrick J. Burke

PATRICK J. BURKE

Patrick Burke, a CPA and attorney, is the managing partner of Burke & Schindler, CPAs, a firm he founded in 1984. Since the firm's inception, Burke has continuously recruited the most talented professionals to broaden the scope of the practice and to ensure Burke & Schindler clients receive top-notch service. The firm specializes in business consulting, taxation, audit and accounting, executive recruiting and staffing, and retirement plan administration.

Burke is a respected expert in business acquisitions and sales, deal structuring, value building and succession planning. In addition, he has advised more than 200 highly successful start-ups. His commitment to a proactive approach has earned him the trust and respect of his clients. He exceeds expectations by becoming clients' go-to business adviser.

Burke has been a featured lecturer on entrepreneurship at The University of Dayton and numerous seminars. He is a former member of the "Forty Under 40" business leaders in Cincinnati and a member of the Ohio Society of Certified Public Accountants, the American Institute of Certified

Public Accountants, the Ohio and American Bar Associations.

Currently, he is Chairman of the board of directors of a closely held $70 million medical consulting company and board member (including chairman of the audit and compensation committees) of a closely held $500 million real estate services business and holds Series 7 and Series 63 licenses.

Burke received his J.D. from the University of Cincinnati Law School and his B.S. cum laude from the University of Dayton.

Outside of work, Patrick is active with Boys Hope Girls Hope of Cincinnati, Catholic Inner City Schools Education Fund (CISE) and The Dynamic Catholic Institute.

If you'd like help buying a business,
running the one you have more profitably,
or selling your business for top dollar,
please contact Patrick Burke:

www.burkecpa.com
901 Adams Crossing
Cincinnati, OH 45202
513-455-8200
business@burkecpa.com